Essential Preparation for

UMAT

UNDERGRADUATE MEDICINE & HEALTH SCIENCES ADMISSION TEST

Series Two

1

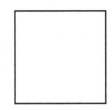

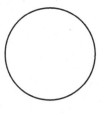

BOOK 1
LOGICAL REASONING
& PROBLEM SOLVING

Mohan Dhall

Five Senses Education Pty Ltd
2/195 Prospect Highway
Seven Hills 2147
New South Wales
Australia

Dhall, Mohan
Series 2, Book 1 - Logical Reasoning & Problem Solving

ISBN 978-1-74130-892-1

CONTENTS

Introduction to UMAT and the Trial Test Papers

Students can gain access into medical training in Australia in one of three ways:

- Through post-graduate entry following the completion of an undergraduate degree. This degree should be in science or science related subjects and the student will need to achieve a high Grade Point Average (GPA)

- Through direct entry based on Year 12 results

- Through the UMAT test and interview

The purpose of an entry test is to assist in the selection of candidates who display the requisite skills and abilities for successful medical training. The three tests: logical reasoning and problem solving, understanding people and non-verbal reasoning assess a range of different types of cognition.

Supplementary to tests is an interview and thus interview skill and techniques should be practiced in addition to students undertaking test-training.

UMAT Trial Examination

Total Test Time: 180 minutes

> **Section 1: 48 Questions (70 minutes)**
>
> **Section 2: 44 Questions (55 minutes)**
>
> **Section 3: 42 Questions (55 minutes)**

This book covers Section 1

Section 1 – Logical Reasoning and Problem Solving (70 minutes)

Number of questions: 48

Time allowed: 70 minutes

Instructions to candidates

Section 1 is a test of logical reasoning and problem-solving. There are 48 questions in this section.

Some of the questions rely on one piece of stimulus information that is provided. This may be presented graphically, in tabular form or in brief text pieces. For each question in this section you are to decide which of the four options given is the correct answer **_based only on the information provided_**.

The questions assess your ability to comprehend, draw logical conclusions, reach solutions by identifying relevant facts, evaluate information, pinpoint additional or missing information, and generate and test plausible hypotheses.

Questions 1 – 2

There has been an ongoing question about just how the Great Pyramid was built by the Ancient Egyptians. With the stone blocks weighing upwards of 2.5 tonnes, various theories have been espoused as to how the stone blocks were moved into place. Amongst the more notable theories are:

- The External Ramp Theory
- Crane Theory
- The Spiral (Internal) Ramp Theory

The External Ramp Theory

This theory has two variations. The first is the straight ramp and the second involves the use of a spiral ramp on the outside of the pyramid. The straight ramp theory posited that a long straight ramp was built, with a gradient of no more than 8^0. At this gradient the ramp would have been over 1.5km long and also would have had to have been periodically raised as the pyramid got taller. The movement of the stones would have been along the top of 'rolling logs'. No evidence of any such ramp has been found, nor has the construction of a ramp like this been thought feasible.

A variation on this theory is that a spiral ramp was built on the outside of the pyramid. The external ramp theory would require that the corners of the pyramid be built last and also that the load was evenly spread at all times. However, as the measurement of the angles would have been required throughout construction, being obscured by a ramp would have made this task impossible.

Crane Theory

Based on the machines made by Herodotus, a shadouf (or long, pivoted lever), various wooden wedges and a system of wooden pegs could all be used to manoeuver the large blocks into place. The work would be very slow, but could be done. However, Egypt does not have the supply of wood that would have been required for the task to be completed.

Spiral (Internal) Ramp Theory

The most accepted theory is that an external ramp was used to build the lower third of the pyramid and that an internal ramp was then used to build the rest. The blocks making up the external ramp would then be used to create the upper two thirds of the pyramid.

The internal ramp was narrower and had a lower gradient (only 7^0) than the external ramp. This would explain why the blocks in the top two-thirds of the pyramid are smaller than the blocks in the lowest third. Further evidence comes in the form of 'corner notches'. Such notches are evidence of the use of cranes outside the pyramid to assist with turning the blocks on the internal ramp at 90^0 when they got to a corner on the narrow internal ramp. The use of microgravimetry, which determines the density of different things based on their gravitational pull, has also confirmed the existence of an internal spiralling ramp.

Question 1

From this information it follows that

A) It would not be possible to build a pyramid using a long straight ramp
B) A combination of a straight and a spiral ramp was probably used
C) Cranes were not essential to the building of the Great Pyramid
D) The external ramp would have reduced pressure on the internal walls

Question 2

If ramps were used then

A) They had to have a gradient of between 7^0 and 90^0
B) They needed to be able to be removed upon completion
C) They had to be made of blocks used within the pyramid
D) The preferred gradient was 8^0

Question 3

There are 86 coloured marbles in a cloth bag. The marble colours are as follows:

- 10 marbles are green
- 7 marbles are red
- 11 marbles are orange
- 8 marbles are blue
- 11 marbles are black
- 17 marbles are purple
- 13 marbles are yellow
- 9 marbles are turquoise

What is the minimum number of marbles that must be taken out of the cloth bag (and not returned to the bag) for a person to be certain that they have drawn out FIVE different coloured marbles?

A) 5 marbles
B) 21 marbles
C) 52 marbles
D) 53 marbles

Questions 4 - 5

Australian scientists have played a key role in developing a diagnostic test for the latest deadly strain of bird flu. With south-east Asia on alert for the H7N9 virus, which has so far killed 32 people, CSIRO's Animal Health Laboratory in Geelong is preparing test kits containing deactivated virus for export to almost a dozen countries. Working with international laboratories, CSIRO scientists developed a blood test which can confirm the presence of the H7N9 strain in ducks or poultry.

Director of the Animal Health Laboratory Kurt Zuelke said the test was developed using a live sample of the virus, which was sent from China in early April. After infecting chickens with the virus to harvest more samples from the infected blood, scientists then irradiated the virus to kill it before it was used as an ingredient in the diagnostic test. "The test contains inactivated virus that is used as a positive control," Dr Zuelke said. "We've grown the virus, irradiated it to kill it and then it can be used as a positive control."

The diagnostic kits have already gone to laboratories in Vietnam, Thailand, Indonesia, Cambodia, Laos and Myanmar. Last week kits containing 8000 tests each were sent to Malaysia, the Philippines and Bangladesh and this week to Nepal and Bhutan. "If or when this new virus starts to circulate beyond China, we have a network across South-East Asia that can detect it as part of their routine surveillance activities," Dr Zuelke said. "The key rationale is to establish an early surveillance network across South-East Asia so that if the virus starts to move, we can respond quickly."

Currently the H7N9 influenza strain has only been reported in China and Taiwan. It has not yet proved transferable from human to human. The World Health Organisation says the H7N9 influenza virus has killed 32 people since February. Another 131 cases have been reported, mostly in eastern China. Scientists in China sequenced the virus' gene earlier this year, making the information available to researchers internationally. "These viruses don't recognise boundaries very well, so it has to be an international effort," Dr Zuelke said.

Adapted from source: http://www.theage.com.au/national/test-hope-for-bird-flu-strain-20130526-2n5at.html#ixzz2UaFeQuB4

Question 4

From the information it follows that

A) The H7N9 virus is transmitted via contact with blood
B) The H7N9 virus is highly likely to spread quickly through South East Asia
C) As the H7N9 virus can be killed by radiation, people with bird flu can be treated with radiation
D) The H7N9 virus is carried by chickens and geese

Question 5

Inactivated viruses

A) Can be used in vaccines
B) Can assist with diagnosis
C) Cannot recognise boundaries between nations or people
D) Cannot have their genes sequenced

Question 6 – 7

De-extinction, or species reconstitution, is a reference to the science of bringing back animals and plants that have become extinct. The possibility of bringing back such animals and plants lies in the science of gene-mapping, DNA sequencing and the use of cloning. For it to be successful there have to be well-preserved samples of DNA.

Successful species revival has occurred, albeit briefly. For example, in 2009, researchers successfully cloned a bucardo (Spanish mountain goat) using DNA taken from the last member of this family of goats before it died in 2000. This was the first cloned animal born from an extinct subspecies. In early 2013, a team at the University of NSW cloned embryos of the gastric-brooding frog (*Rheobatrachus*) which died out in 1983. This ground dwelling frog was named for its reproductive technique of swallowing its eggs, fasting throughout the gestation and birth of the tadpoles within her stomach. The fasting continues for the next week as the tadpoles develop in the mother's stomach. After a week the tadpoles are expelled by her regurgitating all the offspring.

Success in all cases has been mixed: the bucardo, borne by a domestic goat, died within 10 minutes of being born from a lung abnormality and the cloned frog embryos all died within a few days.

Geneticists in Japan said in 2011 they planned to use the DNA from frozen woolly mammoth carcasses to reconstitute the extinct woolly mammoth, which died out about 6,400 years ago during the last Ice Age.

Ethical concerns about species reconstitution include that degraded DNA samples affect the quality of life of the clones. Miscarriage is common in the cloning process and deformity can be a feature of cloned animals. As stated prior, premature death is a feature of cloning. Another concern is that scientists may be focusing on the science of cloning, and successful cloning attempts, rather than the ethics of cloning. Moreover, many species have become extinct on account of loss of habitat and thus if successfully cloned may not have an environment to live in. Moreover, in terms of socialisation, there would be no other animals within the species to help socialise, nurture or teach the cloned animal how to adapt.

Proponents of cloning suggest that apart from reviving lost species, there could also be the restoration of lost habitats, as species could then recreate the environment that had existed at a time when the species survived originally.

© Mohan Dhall
© Five Senses Education Pty Ltd

Question 6

Species reconstitution

A) Is necessary for scientists to understand about lost species
B) Has been successful on two occasions
C) May be possible on account of scientific advances
D) Will be supported when lost habitats are restored

Question 7

Cloning

A) To date has been fraught with complications
B) Inevitably ends in miscarriage or death
C) Will successfully bring back the woolly mammoth
D) Only requires well-preserved samples of DNA

Questions 8 – 10

The information in the Table below relates to the effects of different interventions on muscle and liver glycogen stores. Glycogen is the form in which carbohydrate is stored by the body.

Effects of different interventions on muscle and liver glycogen stores g per kg wet tissue				
Subjects	**Type and time of diet**	**In muscle**	**In liver**	**Total carbohydrate stores (g)**
Untrained	Average (45%) CHO diet	14	54	380
	High (75%) CHO diet	18	70	490
Trained	When training daily (low-CHO diet)	14	30	330
	When training daily (high-CHO diet)	21	70	550
	24-hour fast	21	10	440
	Glycogen stripping (3 days low-CHO diet with exercise)	7	10	158
	Marathon preparation (3 days CHO-loading)	36	90	880
	Immediately post-marathon	4-5	23	130
	24-hours post-race (high-CHO diet)	15	90	460
	48-hours post-race (high-CHO diet)	27	90	700
	1 week post-race (high-CHO diet)	30	90	620

Table 1 Source: T Noakes, The Lore of Running (4th Ed), p 104, OUP, 2003. Notes: CHO = Carbohydrate

Question 8

From the information it can be concluded that

A) More glycogen is always stored in the liver
B) The glycogen stores in the muscles are used up at a greater rate than glycogen stores in the liver
C) After a marathon it takes 24-hours to restore liver glycogen to pre-race levels
D) Glycogen stripping drops glycogen stores to dangerously low levels

Question 9

Which of the following is supported by the information?

A) Untrained people on an average carbohydrate diet have lower amounts of glycogen in the muscles than trained people on a low carbohydrate diet
B) The total carbohydrate stores of an untrained person on a high carbohydrate diet is greater than that of a person with a similar diet who completed a marathon 18-hours ago
C) Carbohydrate loading gives the highest amount of muscle glycogen but the second highest amount of liver glycogen
D) People training for a marathon should not fast beforehand

Question 10

It can be concluded that training

A) increases the liver capacity to store glycogen
B) and also fasting can damage the liver
C) does not decrease the muscle capacity to store glycogen
D) helps the body to adapt to stress

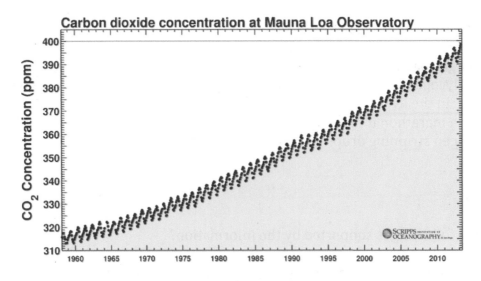

Source: http://keelingcurve.ucsd.edu/

Daily measurements of CO_2 at a US government agency lab on Hawaii have topped 400 parts per million for the first time. The station, which sits on the Mauna Loa volcano, feeds its numbers into a continuous record of the concentration of the gas stretching back to 1958. The last time CO_2 was regularly above 400ppm was three to five million years ago - before modern humans existed. Scientists say the climate back then was also considerably warmer than it is today. Carbon dioxide is regarded as the most important of the manmade greenhouse gases blamed for raising the temperature on the planet over recent decades. Human sources come principally from the burning of fossil fuels such as coal, oil and gas.

Source: http://www.bbc.co.uk/news/science-environment-22486153

Question 11

It can be reliably concluded that

A) CO_2 levels have peaked over the past sixty five years
B) Human activity is causing CO_2 levels to rise
C) The CO_2 levels have risen steadily over the past five million years
D) By 2050 the CO_2 concentration should reach 500 ppm

Question 12

From the information it follows that

A) CO_2 levels peak and then fall by 20ppm in succession
B) CO_2 levels are totally unpredictable
C) CO_2 levels contribute to global warming
D) CO_2 levels rise and fall predictably

Questions 13 – 15

In a select group of persons, exercise can produce a spectrum of allergic symptoms ranging from an *erythematous*, irritating skin eruption to a life-threatening anaphylactic reaction. The differential diagnosis in persons with exercise-induced dermatologic and systemic symptoms should include exercise-induced anaphylaxis and *cholinergic urticaria*. Both are classified as physical allergies. Mast cell degranulation with the release of vasoactive substances appears to be an inciting factor for the production of symptoms in both cases. Exercise-induced anaphylaxis and *cholinergic urticaria* can be differentiated on the basis of urticarial morphology, reproducibility, progression to anaphylaxis and response to passive warming. Diagnosis is usually based on a thorough history and examination of the morphology of the lesions. Management of acute episodes of exercise-induced anaphylaxis includes cessation of exercise, administration of epinephrine and antihistamines, vascular support and airway maintenance. Long-term care may require modification of or abstinence from exercise, avoidance of co-precipitating factors and the prophylactic use of medications such as antihistamines and mast cell stabilisers.

Exercise-induced anaphylaxis is a distinct form of physical allergy and, although rare, has been consistently described in the literature since the 1970s. This disorder is classically characterised by a spectrum of symptoms occurring during physical activity that ranges from mild cutaneous signs to severe systemic manifestations such as hypotension, syncope and even death.

Exercise-induced anaphylaxis has been described at all levels of physical exertion and during various athletic activities. In susceptible persons, ingestion of certain foods or medications before physical activity may be a predisposing factor. Aspirin and nonsteroidal anti-inflammatory drugs (NSAIDs) have been the most frequently implicated medications. Foods that have been implicated include seafood, celery, wheat and cheese. A variant has been described in which seven members of the same family exhibited exercise-induced cutaneous, respiratory and occasional vascular symptoms that were attributed to exercise-induced anaphylaxis.

Because symptoms may vary greatly, many persons with exercise-induced anaphylaxis are unaware of their condition. Similarly, because it is a relatively rare condition, it often goes undiagnosed. Primary care physicians should be able to recognise and manage exercise-induced anaphylaxis and help patients prevent the condition.

Source: http://www.aafp.org/afp/2001/1015/p1367.html

Question 13

From the information, the management of exercise induced anaphylaxis does NOT include

    A) Refraining from exercise
    B) Using antihistamines
    C) Avoiding particular foods
    D) Performing very low intensity exercises

Question 14

It can be concluded that

    A) Four factors are responsible for exercise induced anaphylaxis
    B) People should not eat before they exercise
    C) Lumps under the skin can occur from exercise
    D) Itchy skin follows periods of strong exercise

Question 15

Exercise induced anaphylaxis and *cholinergic urticaria*

    A) Occur in those who are susceptible to exercise-induced allergy
    B) Requires the use of an epipen in its management
    C) Are both allergies caused by aerobic activity
    D) Are different but manifest with similar symptoms

Questions 16 - 18

Internationally, approximately 371 million people are living with diabetes - 90% of these cases are type 2 diabetes. By the year 2030, there will be an estimated 550 million people with diabetes if this progression continues. Since 1980, cases of diabetes have increased twofold - with 70 percent of the change happening because of aging populations around the world - while the other 30 percent are due to the rising incidence of risk factors, including obesity.

Obesity is well-known known as a risk factor for type 2 diabetes. Recently a key mechanism has been found in the immune system that plays a part in the development of obesity-linked type 2 diabetes. Previous research has shown the link between obesity and diabetes, but the molecules that cause this link have been a mystery. The investigators studied mice that were genetically engineered to not have T-bet, a protein that controls the differentiation and function of immune cells. Researchers found that the mice had heightened insulin sensitivity, even though they were obese.

The researchers found that the intra-abdominal fat of these mice had fewer immune cells and was less swollen than that of regular mice. They further discovered that by moving immune cells that had no T-bet to younger, skinnier mice, the insulin sensitivity improved. It appears that T-bet expression in the adaptive immune system is able to influence metabolic physiology.

Generally, obesity is linked to insulin resistance and diabetes, however, this is not always the case. Many of the most common medications used to treat type 2 diabetes function by improving insulin sensitivity. More trials are needed to pinpoint other molecules in the pathway of action of T-bet, which could start the process for future drug options for the treatment of type 2 diabetes. Giving specific immune cells as immunotherapy to better insulin resistance could also be a possibility for therapy in the future.

Additional information

Overweight and obesity are defined as abnormal or excessive fat accumulation that may impair health. Body mass index (BMI) is a simple index of weight-for-height that is commonly used to classify overweight and obesity in adults. It is defined as a person's weight in kilograms divided by the square of his height in metres (kg/m^2).

The WHO definition is:

- a BMI greater than or equal to 25 is overweight
- a BMI greater than or equal to 30 is obesity.

Overweight and obesity are the fifth leading risk for global deaths. At least 2.8 million adults die each year as a result of being overweight or obese. In addition, 44% of the diabetes burden, 23% of the ischaemic heart disease burden and between 7% and 41% of certain cancer burdens are attributable to overweight and obesity.

Source of additional data: http://www.who.int/mediacentre/factsheets/fs311/en/

Question 16

From the information

A) The causes of diabetes are people living longer and having a BMI of 30+
B) About a quarter of people who are obese die of diabetes annually
C) Type 2 diabetes is more prevalent than ischaemic heart disease
D) Thirty percent of the increase in diabetes has come from obesity

Question 17

It can be concluded that

A) Insulin sensitivity is low in obese persons
B) Type 2 diabetes is best treated with drugs that adapt to insulin
C) Removal of the T-bet protein increases insulin sensitivity
D) Increasing insulin sensitivity will overcome diabetes in thin mice

Question 18

From the information it follows that

A) A BMI of 24% is unhealthy
B) Treating the cause of obesity will reduce the incidence of cancers
C) A person weighing 40kg who is 1 metre tall is obese
D) Obese mice will have a higher incidence of ischaemic heart disease

Questions 19 - 20

In the town of Ajara there are 6,000 adults, two fifths of whom are female. 45% of males work in factories and 20% of the females work in offices. 40% of adults own cars. 1,800 adults own cars and are employed either in factories or offices.

Question 19

How many adults own cars and do not work in factories or offices?

A) 4,200
B) 600
C) 300
D) 480

Question 20

If 80% of the adult population works, then what proportion works in factories and offices?

A) $^{13}/_{20}$
B) $^{13}/_{16}$
C) $^{9}/_{16}$
D) $^{7}/_{16}$

Questions 21 - 22

Very small amounts of magnetite (also called 'lodestone') has been found on the beaks of pigeons. It has been found that exposure to a magnet can disorientate a pigeon and that one attached to a pigeon can make it lose its way. Similarly, bees exposed to strong magnets become disorientated and cannot find their way back to their own hive, even when it is nearby.

Migratory animals such as swallows, salmon, dolphins, turtles, monarch butterflies and stingray have sensory cells that also carry traces of magnetite, Fe_3O_4. The magnetite crystals can be as small as 280 angstroms in size. An angstrom is 10^{-10} of a metre (one billionth of a metre). It is understood that the magnetite gives creatures the capacity for homing and finding out where they are, using the Earths geomagnetic fields. This is different to a GPS* system based on satellite imaging.

Under electron microscopy it has become clear that there is an interaction within bees, and other creatures with the homing instinct, between trophocytes (nutritive cells that happen to contain magnetite in creatures that can navigate) and the nervous system. In this way the cells call act as receptors to detect magnetism. These receptors are finely sensitised to changes in the Earth's magnetic fields. Changes can arise spasmodically and for a temporary period when there are very large solar flares

* GPS Global Positioning Satellite

Question 21

It can be concluded that

    A) Flying close to electrical wires can disorientate pigeons
    B) Without iron in their diets homing pigeons would not be able to fly home
    C) Solar flares may disrupt the flight of bees
    D) Pigeons that eat bees will have a stronger sense of where they are

Question 22

From the information

    A) Trophocytes and the nervous system work together to help orientate
    B) Pain receptors and trophocytes are closely matched in the body
    C) Trophocytes must work with the circulatory system for a creature to be able to perceive position
    D) Receptors in the nervous system can act independently of trophocytes

Questions 23 - 24

There are currently over one million feral camels and this population will double in the next 8-10 years and beyond. At this population level feral camels are having significant negative impacts across their extensive range and are expanding into new areas. These impacts are environmental, social, cultural and economic. The overarching challenges for the National Plan are to set a framework that will enable rapid and humane reduction of the currently over-abundant feral camel population to a level where it does not threaten the integrity of assets and social values and where jurisdictions and landowners can readily undertake on-going management to protect these assets and values, and ensure there is a legacy or platform in place that will sustain on-going protection of these assets and values from feral camels. These central challenges are complicated by the array of other challenges that the implementation of the National Plan faces.

The feral camel range extends across three states (Western Australia, South Australia, Queensland) and the Northern Territory. Each jurisdiction has legislative and regulatory frameworks for the management of all pest animals including feral camels, which landholders must abide by. However, the detailed requirements of these frameworks have not been harmonised across jurisdictional boundaries. To date there has been little cooperative, cross-jurisdictional feral camel management except on a small scale *ad hoc* basis. This limited cross-jurisdictional effort has had little impact on feral camel populations overall, and has been ineffective in mitigating their impacts across Australia's rangelands. The jurisdictions are facing a considerable challenge to:

- harmonise legislative and regulatory requirements for feral camel control, and/or
- develop appropriate protocols to both allow and encourage cross jurisdictional
- feral camel management, and
- implement mechanisms to deal with the management of feral camels across different land tenures (e.g. pastoral, government and Aboriginal) when the approach required needs to access all tenures.

The values that are held by individuals and stakeholder groups about feral camels vary considerably. For some groups the negative impacts that feral camels have on environmental, social and cultural values are highly significant. Similarly, the economic costs associated with damage to infrastructure (such as fences) caused by feral camels and expenditure required to manage feral camels is a significant impost to land managers. Alternatively some communities and individuals see that feral camels are a potential economic resource that could be harnessed providing local employment and income. Further, the value of feral camels as a protein resource that could contribute towards a need in the world context is also valued by some individuals and groups.

Source: http://www.environment.gov.au/biodiversity/invasive/publications/pubs/feral-camel-action-plan.pdf

Question 23

From the information

   A) Aligning state-based responses would be beneficial to the management of feral camels
   B) Reducing the scale of interaction between the states would have a big impact on the feral camel problem
   C) Aboriginal communities must learn to manage the issues arising from free-roaming feral camels
   D) Camels are a valuable source of food for many Australians

Question 24

Feral camels

   A) Have overwhelmingly negative economic and social impacts
   B) Can have beneficial economics impacts if well-managed
   C) Are treated differently by pastoralists, government and Aboriginal Australians
   D) Damage fences and other infrastructure like roads

Questions 25 – 28

The 121,752 marriages registered in 2011 represented an increase of 576 (0.5%) from the 121,176 marriages registered in Australia in 2010. In 2011, there were 48,935 divorces granted in Australia, a decrease of 1,305 (2.6%) compared to 2010.

Total marriages, Australia - 1991-2011

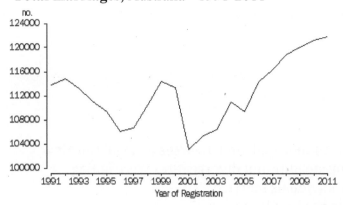

Total divorces granted, Australia - 1991-2011

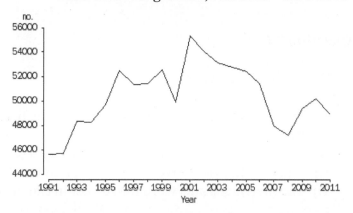

Between 2001 and 2006, the census count in *de facto* relationships rose by 25% from 951,500 to 1,193,400. This was lower than the increase between 1996 and 2001 (28%).

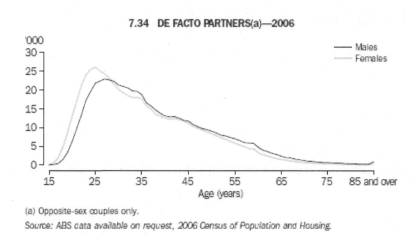

7.34 DE FACTO PARTNERS(a)—2006

(a) Opposite-sex couples only.
Source: ABS data available on request, 2006 Census of Population and Housing.

Sources: www.abs.gov.au

Question 25

From the information it is evident that

A) Marriage rates have risen steadily since 2001
B) Divorce rates peaked when the marriage rate peaked
C) In 2008 the number of marriages rose to above the 1999 levels
D) During the GFC of 2008 – 2010 divorce rates fell

Question 26

In 2011

A) Marriage registrations were at an all time high and divorces at an all time low
B) Marriage registrations were rising steadily and divorce rates were falling
C) More individuals divorced than individuals married
D) 756 more couples married than in the previous year

Question 27

2001 is anomalous because

A) The marriage rates were the lowest in the decade and the divorce rates were rising
B) The marriage rates were the lowest on record and the divorce rates peaked
C) The marriage rates were the falling and the divorce rates were rising
D) The marriage rates were the lowest in the decade and the divorce rates peaked

Question 28

Which of the following is true?

A) The increase in *de facto* relationships between 2001 and 2006 was matched by a rise in marriages and also divorces
B) In 2006 the number if males aged 25-years in *de facto* relationships was higher than the number of females aged 30 in *de facto* relationships
C) There is a close correlation between the rise in divorce rates and the rise in number of *de facto* couples
D) In 2006 there were 1,193,400 *de facto* relationships, 115,000 marriages and 51,600 divorces

Effect of Microgravity on the Peripheral Subcutaneous Veno-Arteriolar Reflex in Humans (Xenon1)

Description

When the body's legs are lower in relationship to the heart, the body triggers what is called a local veno-arteriolar reflex, where small subcutaneous (below the surface of the skin) blood vessels constrict, forcing blood from the feet toward the head. If this reflex is not properly triggered or if blood circulation is impeded, the blood pressure drops, causing dizziness and, possibly, fainting. This effect is called orthostatic intolerance. Due to a number of possible reasons - reduced fluid volume, muscle atrophy, neurovestibular adaptation - astronauts suffer from orthostatic intolerance during entry and landing, and for a few days postflight, potentially interfering with their ability to perform entry and landing tasks and prolonging their recovery period. Xenon-1 tested the local veno-arteriolar reflex in an effort to understand the source of, and ways to combat, postflight orthostatic intolerance.

Prior to and following Expeditions 3, 4, and 5, station crewmembers were placed on a gurney as a small amount of Xenon-133, a radioactive isotope dissolved in sterile saline solution, was injected into the subcutaneous tissue of their lower legs. Arterial blood pressure was recorded by a continuous pressure device on the crewmember's index finger. This measurement, which was taken with the Xenon-1 detector unit, was used to trace the movement of the Xenon tracer following injection. As the measurements were taken, the Xenon memory box recorded and displayed the counting rate.

Space Applications

While a person is standing (orthostasis), blood has a tendency to pool in the legs and feet. This collecting of blood in the lower body can lead to a blood pressure drop in the upper body, and if less blood gets to the brain, the astronauts may experience dizziness or fainting. It is a condition called orthostatic intolerance, and it can affect astronauts for several days after returning from space. The veno-arteriolar (V-A) reflex acts together with other reflexes to prevent this. When blood pooling is detected in the lower limbs, the V-A reflex constricts blood vessels just below the skin (subcutaneous vessels) to prevent edema and pooling of blood and thereby maintain blood pressure and blood supply to the brain. Treatments for this condition are currently under investigation (one is the drug Midodrine, which is being tested by ISS astronauts). The exact mechanism that creates orthostatic intolerance is still not completely understood. This study's method of visualizing blood flow will allow the roles of the subcutaneous vessels and the V-A reflex to be characterized, allowing for possible treatments in the future.

Source: http://www.nasa.gov/mission_pages/station/research/experiments/301.html#description

Question 29

From this information

A) Veno-arteriolar reflex involves dilation of the subcutaneous blood vessels
B) Veno-arteriolar reflex works by itself to overcome orthostatic intolerance
C) Subcutaneous vessels do not constrict when astronauts enter the atmosphere
D) Postflight orthostatic intolerance is detected through use of a sterile solution

Question 30

It can be concluded that the effects of orthostatic intolerance include

A) Pooling of blood in the legs and blotchiness to the hands and face
B) Dizziness, migrane and fainting
C) Fainting, dizziness and temporary hearing loss
D) Blood pressure drop in the upper body, fainting and dizziness

Questions 31 - 32

Nutrition Information							
Servings per package: 11				**Serving size 18.3g (1 biscuit)**			
	Quantity Per serving	% Daily Intake* Per Serving	Quantity Per 100g		Quantity Per serving	% Daily Intake* Per Serving	Quantity Per 100g
Energy	399kJ	4.6%	2180kJ	Carbohydrate	11.8g	3.8%	64.4g
Protein	0.9g	1.8%	4.8g	- Sugars	8.1g	9.0%	44.2g
Fat, Total	4.9g	7.0%	27.0g	Sodium	29mg	1.3%	160mg
- Saturated	2.7g	11.3%	14.9g				

* Percentage daily intakes are based on an average adult diet of 8,700kJ

Question 31

36.6 grams of the food would provide

A) about 9% of the daily energy intake
B) about 30% of the daily energy intake
C) 3.8% of the daily energy intake
D) about 14% of the daily energy intake

Question 32

3 serves

A) would weigh 54.9g and provide 3.7% of daily sodium requirements
B) would equal 27.3% of the package and would provide 24.3g of sugars
C) would provide just over $1/5$ of daily total fat and just under 10% of daily carbohydrates
D) would provide 480mg of sodium and 35.4g of carbohydrate

Indigenous Group	Location	Months of the calendar year											
		J	F	M	A	M	J	J	A	S	O	N	D
Brambuk	Halls Gap, Victoria	Late summer - Hot, dry days		Autumn - Cool mornings		Winter - Bleak mists	Pre-Spring - Wettest months			Spring - Warmer days		Early summer - Weather stabilises	
D'harwal	Sydney Basin	Bhuran - Hot and dry			Marrai'gang - Wet becoming cooler		Burrugin - cold, frosty, short days		Wiritjiribin - cold and windy	Ngoonungi - cool getting warmer	Parra'dowee - Warm and wet		
Jawoyn	Northern Territory	Jiorrk - Wet rains		Bungarung - Last rains	Jungalk - Early hot dry		Malaparr - Middle dry			Worrwopmi - Hot and sticky		Wakkaringding - First rains	
Mirriwoong	West Australia	Nyinggiyi-mageny - Wet			Warnka-mageny - Cold					Barndenyirriny - Hot			Nyinggiyi-mageny - Wet
Walabunba	Central Australia	Wantangka - Hot and wet			Yurluurrp - Cool and dry							Wantangka - Hot and wet	
Wardaman	Northern Territory	Yijilg - Wet	Wulujujun - Last of the rains		Wujerrijin - Dry and cold						Ngurruwan - Hot and dry, rains begin		Yijilg - Wet
Yanyuwa	Gulf of Carpenteria	Wunthurru - Early rains		Lhabayi - Wet season, heavy rainfall		Rra-mardu - Dry season, dews and fogs			Ngardaru - hot, dusty	Na-yinarramba - Hot and humid			
Yawuru	North West, Western Australia	Mankala - Wet season			Marul - Hot and still	Wirralburru - Cool and dry	Barrgana - Cold, fog, dust storms			Wirlburu – Cool, dry, dusty	Larja - Hot, humid		Mankala - Wet season

Question 33

Indigenous Australian groups

A) Had a Eurocentric understanding of the four seasons
B) Described the seasons in terms of heat/cold/wet/dusty and dry
C) Described climate similarly in all Australian jurisdictions
D) Classified the annual climate as having between 3 and 7 seasons

Question 34

The Yawuru and the Mirriwoong peoples

A) Had a largely similar set of climate descriptors
B) Demonstrate that even within one State the climate can vary markedly
C) Both describe December as wet and September as hot and dusty
D) Follow similar climate classifications as the Yanyuwa and Walabunba peoples

Question 35

Which of the following is true?

A) Six months after the start of the Marrai'gang the climate is cold and wet
B) Four months prior to the start of Wujerrijin it is wet and hot
C) Three months after the start of the Wunthurru it is hot and humid
D) Four months after the end of the Ngoonungi there are dust storms

Questions 36 - 38

The amount of any gas that can be dissolved in a liquid depends on the partial pressure of the gas over the solution and the nature and temperature of the liquid. If you increase the pressure of the gas, more gas will dissolve in solution. Another factor relevant is time: The longer you are at a given depth (pressure), the more nitrogen will dissolve in solution. Underwater, your body must deal with two major issues: pressure and temperature. Pressure affects the amount of nitrogen and oxygen gases that dissolve in your blood and tissues. Pressure also affects your ears and sinuses. The ability of water to absorb your body heat can lower your body temperature and put you at risk for hypothermia.

The air we breathe is a mixture of mostly nitrogen (78 percent) and some oxygen (21 percent). When you inhale air, your body consumes the oxygen, replaces some of it with carbon dioxide and does nothing with the nitrogen. At normal atmospheric pressure, some nitrogen and oxygen is dissolved in the fluid portions of your blood and tissues. As you descend under the water, the pressure on your body increases, so more nitrogen and oxygen dissolve in your blood. Most of the oxygen gets consumed by your tissues, but the nitrogen remains dissolved. Increased nitrogen pressure has two problematic effects on your body: nitrogen narcosis and residual nitrogen.

First, when the nitrogen partial pressure reaches high levels, usually those experienced when you reach depths of about 30m or more, you experience a feeling of euphoria called nitrogen narcosis. Nitrogen narcosis can impair your judgement and make you feel relaxed or even sleepy. Narcosis comes on suddenly and without warning, but can be relieved by ascending to a shallower depth because the nitrogen starts to come out of solution as pressure decreases.

Second, the amount of excess nitrogen in your tissues depends on how deep you dive and the amount of time you spend at those depths. The only way that you can rid your body of residual nitrogen, excess nitrogen in your tissues, is to ascend to the surface, which relieves the pressure and allows the nitrogen to come out of solution. If you ascend slowly, the nitrogen comes out of solution slowly. In contrast, if you ascend rapidly, the nitrogen comes out of your blood quickly, forming bubbles. When nitrogen bubbles form in your system, a condition known as decompression sickness or "the bends", they block tiny blood vessels. This can lead to heart attacks, strokes, ruptured blood vessels in the lungs and joint pain (one of the first symptoms of decompression sickness is a "tingling" sensation in your limbs). The best way to avoid decompression sickness is to minimize residual nitrogen by adhering to the "no decompression" depths. If you violate the "no decompression" limits, you have to stay underwater longer, for various times at pre-set depths to allow the nitrogen to come out of your system slowly. This can present problems because you're dealing with a limited air supply; and if you ignore the decompression guidelines, you will suffer "the bends," have to be airlifted to a decompression chamber and be decompressed under emergency medical conditions. It's a life-threatening situation.

Source: http://adventure.howstuffworks.com/outdoor-activities/water-sports/scuba3.htm

Question 36

It can be concluded that at a depth of 35m underwater

A) A diver can get hypothermia and decompression sickness
B) A diver can feel drowsy and euphoric
C) A diver is at risk of death and should ascend quickly
D) A diver's blood oxygen concentration is low

Question 37

Nitrogen narcosis and residual nitrogen

A) Can both be managed by decreasing dive depth
B) Result in heart attack, stroke and ruptured blood vessels
C) Can be overcome by rapidly ascending to the surface of the water
D) Require management through use of a decompression chamber

Question 38

A significant risk of diving at depth is

A) The danger presented by compression and subsequent decompression
B) Temperature loss and the numbing effect this has on the lungs
C) The need to lower dissolved nitrogen levels and manage a limited air supply
D) A "tingling" sensation in the limbs, signifying nitrogen narcosis

Questions 39 - 40

Scientific name: *Rheobatrachus silus*
Common name: Southern Gastric-brooding Frog

Life Cycle

Breeding activity for the Southern Gastric-brooding Frog occured between October and December and appeared to be dependent on summer rains (Ingram 1983). The species featured a unique reproductive mode in which eggs or early larvae were swallowed by the female and completed their development in the stomach (Tyler & Carter 1982). Hormones produced by the young inhibited the digestive secretions of the stomach and rendered the upper intestine inactive (Tyler et al. 1983).

The larvae relied on yolk reserves throughout development. Up to 25 young were brooded in each event and emerged from the mother's mouth as fully formed metamorphs at about six to seven weeks. The digestive tract returned to its normal state and the female recommenced feeding within four days of releasing the young (Tyler & Davies 1983b).

The brooding periods from two individuals of 36 and 43 days suggest that the duration was such that females were unlikely to breed twice in one season (Ingram 1983).

Feeding

The Southern Gastric-brooding Frog was observed to forage and take insects from both land and water (Ingram 1983). In an aquarium situation *Lepidoptera*, *Diptera* and *Neuroptera* were eaten (Liem 1973).

Movement Patterns

The Southern Gastric-brooding Frog was an aquatic species that was never recorded more than four metres from water (Ingram 1983). Males, females and juveniles appeared to have limited home ranges, although juveniles and gravid females were particularly mobile (females carrying young tended to be sedentary). Only two juveniles out of ten were found to have moved more than three metres between observations. Juveniles were mobile in the sense that they would move to newly created pools, but once stationed there they usually remained in that area. During a breeding season, the home range of females and males was estimated to be 0–3.4 m (n=4) and 0.6–2m (n=10) respectively.

Source: http://www.environment.gov.au/cgi-bin/sprat/public/publicspecies.pl?taxon_id=1909

Question 39

Without rain the Gastric-brooding Frog

A) Will not move more than 4 metres from water
B) Will not reproduce
C) Will not breed more than twice in the season
D) Cannot move between adjacent pools

Question 40

The tadpoles of the Gastric-Brooding Frog

A) Did not get digested as secreted hormones inhibit digestive secretions
B) Would form groups of up to 25 and would be 'externally born' together after six weeks
C) Eat insects from land and water
D) Moved further than juveniles did

Questions 41 – 42

<u>Hyperbaric Oxygen Therapy (HBOT)</u>

Hyperbaric literally translates to 'over pressure'. HBOT exposes the patient to higher than normal pressure while the patient breathes 100% oxygen. This can only be achieved in a pressurised vessel (hyperbaric chamber). Breathing pure oxygen while in a pressurised environment results in therapeutic effects for the patient. Hyperbaric treatments for wounds occur at pressures between 2.0 and 2.4 times the pressure at sea level. In real terms, this delivers up to 15 times the normal level of oxygen to the body; this can only be achieved in a hyperbaric chamber, and causes some important changes in the body. HBOT has many benefits in wound healing.

HBOT can overcome areas of poor oxygenation. This is particularly true for parts of the body that have poor small vessel circulation (such as in people with diabetes). Oxygen at higher concentrations can supply the most distant tissues (such as skin on the toes) with the vital building blocks required to help repair damage. In turn, this reduces the need for more radical treatment such as surgery and potentially amputation. This process is called *angioneogenesis* ('new blood vessel growth'). This takes between 15 and 40 treatments to work and new small blood vessels can be grown within tissues with degraded blood vessels. This is a particular problem for people with diabetes and people who have had radiotherapy for cancers. The former may develop wounds that do not heal, leading to amputations, while the latter can have problems such as bleeding bowels, bladders or a breakdown of normal tissues in the areas where they have received radiotherapy.

Infections are naturally attacked by the body's white blood cells that use chemicals to destroy bacteria and are rapidly broken down to limit the damage to normal tissues. Some of these chemicals are called *'reactive oxygen species'* and include chemicals such as hydrogen peroxide (H_2O_2). For the white cells to work properly they need oxygen to convert into these natural 'antibiotics' and the additional oxygen delivered by HBOT optimises this effect. High levels of oxygen can also deactivate some of the toxins that are produced by bacteria, particularly in gas gangrene, reducing the infection's ability to spread.

Wound healing is a complex process. Several stages of the wound-healing process require a good level of oxygen for cells to build the structure around which the wound can heal. In some conditions (such as diabetes or auto-immune diseases) the reduced delivery of oxygen creates a weak healing process 'scaffold' which leads to recurrence of the wound or a wound that does not heal at all. Conversely, an increased delivery of oxygen provides a strong healing 'scaffold' and fights infection, resulting in complete and proper healing of the wound.

Source: http://www.hyperbarichealth.com/doc/hyperbarichealth-booklet.pdf

Question 41

It can be concluded that breathing pure oxygen while at pressure

A) Will assist in the production of hydrogen peroxide to bleach infection and kill it
B) Encourages the development of healing scaffolds that benefit diabetes and cancer sufferers
C) Encourages the capacity for small blood vessels to carry oxygen thus assisting in the repair of extremities
D) Repairs degraded blood vessels and also creates an intricate network of new blood vessels

Question 42

Wounds

A) Occurring at pressures of between 2.0 and 2.4 times the atmospheric pressure at sea level can be treated through HBOT
B) Treated through HBOT at pressures of over 2.4 times the atmospheric pressure at sea level would heal over 15 times faster
C) That do not heal through conventional means should be treated with oxygen under a pressure of between 2.0 and 2.4 times the atmospheric pressure at sea level
D) Can receive oxygen at a concentration 15 times higher through HBOT than treatment outside of a pressurised, pure-oxygen environment

Questions 43 and 44

Autoimmune diseases are characterised by the body's immune responses being directed against its own tissues, causing prolonged inflammation and subsequent tissue destruction. Autoimmune disorders can either cause immune-responsive cells to attack the linings of the joints (resulting in rheumatoid arthritis) or trigger immune cells to attack the insulin-producing islet cells of the pancreas (leading to insulin-dependent diabetes mellitus).

A healthy immune system recognises, identifies, remembers, attacks, and destroys bacteria, viruses, fungi, parasites, cancer cells, or any health-damaging agents not normally present in the body. A defective immune system wreaks havoc throughout the host by directing antibodies against its own tissues.

Any disease in which cytotoxic cells are directed against self-antigens in the body's tissues is considered autoimmune in nature. Such diseases include but are not limited to Celiac disease, Crohn's disease, pancreatitis, systemic lupus erythematosus, Sjogren's syndrome, Hashimoto's thyroiditis and other endocrinopathies. Allergies and multiple sclerosis are also the result of disordered immune functioning.

Source: http://www.lef.org/protocols/immune_connective_joint/autoimmune_diseases_01.htm

Question 43

It can be concluded that

- A) Celiac disease is characterised by cytotoxic cells attacking the body's own tissues
- B) In rheumatoid arthritis the body's joint cells attack the immune cells
- C) A healthy immune system will effectively fight off pancreatitis once it has been contracted
- D) Inflammation in the body is a result of an autoimmune response

Questions 44

It follows that

- A) Protective immunity and autoimmunity result from similar biological responses
- B) An effective autoimmune response occurs when cytotoxic cells are killed by the bodies antigens
- C) Graves' disease must be autoimmune in nature because it is characterised by the production of antibodies to the thyroid-stimulating hormone (TSH) receptor in the thyroid gland
- D) Bacteria, fungi and virus causing agents trigger a defective immune response in otherwise healthy bodies

Questions 45 – 46

Weekly forecast for London Friday 31 May – Thursday 6 June 2013

Friday	Saturday	Sunday	Monday	Tuesday	Wednesday	Thursday
Hi: 21 °C Lo: 10 °C	Hi: 18 °C Lo: 9 °C	Hi: 18 °C Lo: 10 °C	Hi: 19 °C Lo: 8 °C	Hi: 20 °C Lo: 9 °C	Hi: 20 °C Lo: 11 °C	Hi: 21 °C Lo: 10 °C

48-hour forecast for London: Thursday 30 May 2013 – Saturday 1 June 2013

Thursday		Friday				Saturday
Afternoon	Evening	Night	Morning	Afternoon	Evening	Night
14 °C	15 °C	10 °C	10 °C	21 °C	18 °C	12 °C
18 km/h ↓	16 km/h ↓	15 km/h ↓	17 km/h ↘	16 km/h ↘	10 km/h ↘	14 km/h ↘

Sunrise at 4:51 AM in direction 52° Northeast ↗

Sunset at 9:06 PM in direction 308° Northwest ↖

Source: http://www.timeanddate.com/worldclock/city.html?n=136

Question 45

It can be concluded that

A) From Thursday to Saturday the winds shift from the North to the North East and
   the temperature rises
B) The wind shifts Easterly over time and precipitation increases
C) The skies are clear for the week
D) Humidity rises on Sunday, Monday, Tuesday and Thursday

Question 46

It follows that

A) Sunrise should be later than 4.51am on Sunday
B) Sunset should be earlier than 9.06pm on Monday
C) Sunset will be earlier than 4.51am a fortnight from Sunday
D) Sunrise should be at 4.51am and sunset at 9.06pm on Saturday

Questions 47 - 48

Key findings of the *D&B Business Failures and Start-ups Analysis* for the December quarter 2011 are:

- Nationwide, insolvencies rose 42 per cent year-on-year while the number of new businesses fell 11 per cent over the same period;
- Small business failures grew 57 per cent over the year among firms with less than five employees and 40 per cent over the year among firms with six to 19 employees;
- Small business start-ups among firms with less than five employees fell 95 per cent in the year;
- Failures were most pronounced within the service (up 58%), finance (up 58%) and construction (up 66%) sectors; and
- Start-ups during the December quarter in the manufacturing, service and finance sectors fell by nearly 100 per cent.

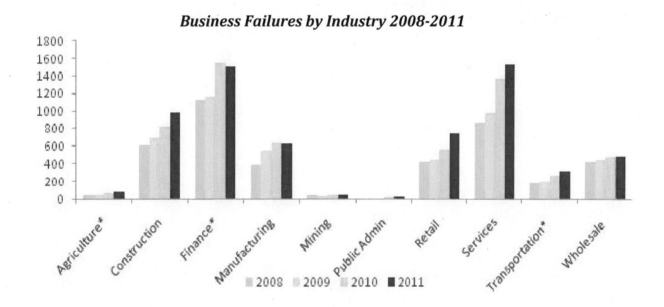

Business Failures by Industry 2008-2011

Source: http://dnbsmallbusiness.com.au/News/Small_business_failures_up_48_per_cent/indexdl_8157.aspx

Question 47

It can be concluded that over the period 2008-11

A) Businesses in the finance industry experienced higher closure rates that any other industry
B) The effects of the economic downturn in 2010 impacted more financial businesses than services and retail businesses combined
C) Over 4,000 businesses across all industries failed in 2009
D) Mining and manufacturing firms went against trend in 2011

Question 48

When there is business closures it can be concluded that

A) There are fewer people prepared to set up their own small business
B) Business owners need more finance to set up than at other times
C) The risk of failure increases by over 50%
D) Only the largest businesses survive

ANSWERS
Summary & Worked Solutions
Multiple Choice Answer Sheet

Logical Reasoning Answers

1	B	17	C	33	D
2	A	18	C	34	B
3	D	19	B	35	B
4	D	20	D	36	B
5	B	21	C	37	A
6	C	22	A	38	C
7	A	23	A	39	B
8	C	24	B	40	A
9	B	25	C	41	C
10	C	26	B	42	D
11	A	27	D	43	A
12	D	28	D	44	C
13	D	29	C	45	B
14	C	30	D	46	C
15	D	31	A	47	C
16	A	32	B	48	A

A = 11
B = 12
C = 14
D = 11

Answers

Question 1

B

A is possible, though it did not happen. Cranes were used as evidenced by notches on the corners, thus C is incorrect. There is no evidence to suggest that the external ramp would have reduced pressure – rather it would have increased pressure.

Thus B is correct.

Question 2

A

The text says that the gradient of the inner ramp was 7° and that the gradient of the external ramp was higher (though unspecified). Thus it can be concluded that the ramps were between 7° and 90° hence A is correct.

Question 3

D

To be assured of getting five different coloured marbles it must be assumed that ALL of each colour for the four most prevalent colours are drawn in full, first. Though this is unlikely it is possible. Hence the number of draws must be: 17 + 13 +11 + 11 (all of the four most occurring colours) + 1 (the first of a fifth colour) = 53 marbles. Hence D is correct.

Question 4

D

There is no evidence to suggest that the H7N9 virus is transmitted by contact with blood so A can be ruled out. There is no evidence to suggest the virus will be spread quickly anywhere so B can also be discounted. Whilst the virus may be killed by radiation it does not follow that people with the virus must receive radiation treatment hence C is not right either. The virus is carried by poultry and thus chicken and geese can be carriers so D is correct.

Question 5

B

The killed virus is being used as a control in diagnostic tests and thus can assist with diagnosis. There is no evidence to suggest that A is true. C is irrelevant and D does not follow from the excerpt, thus B is correct.

Question 6

C

Species reconstitution is not necessary for scientist to understand about lost species as species that are known are currently being lost. Moreover, it does not follow that reconstitution will given insight into what has been lost. Hence A cannot be correct. There have been several or numerous successful attempts at species reconstitution thus B is not correct. Lost habitat, it is suggested may be restored if species are reconstituted – not the other way around, hence D is not correct.

C is correct as the article is all about the possibilities arising from scientific advances.

Question 7

A

There have been no really successful cloned species. Whilst to date there has been miscarriage and death – it does not follow that there always will be. It certainly is not clear that a woolly mammoth will be reconstituted or that this would even be desirable. Thus B and C are clearly incorrect.

Well preserved DNA samples are necessary – but not the ONLY thing – required for successful species reconstitution. Hence D is wrong and A is correct

Question 8

C

During a 24-hour fast there is more glycogen stored in the muscles than the liver thus A is incorrect. The rate at which glycogen is used is not referred to hence B is not correct. Glycogen stripping does drop glycogen levels but there is no evidence that this is dangerous – thus D is not correct either.

From the table it can be seen that within 24-hours of completing a marathon the liver stores rise to 90g per kg of wet tissue, hence C is correct.

Question 9

B

A is not correct as the average muscle glycogen stores in untrained people on an average carbohydrate diet is exactly the same as that of trained people on a low-CHO diet: 14g per kg of wet tissue. Carbohydrate loading gives the highest amount of muscle glycogen (36g per kg of wet tissue) and the equal highest amount of liver glycogen (90g per kg of wet tissue) thus C is not correct.
There is no evidence from the table of fasting affecting marathoners thus D is not correct.

B is correct as at 18g per kg of wet tissue a person on a high CHO diet has greater levels of muscle glycogen than a marathon runner on the same diet 24-hours after a marathon (15g per kg of wet tissue).

Question 10

C

A is not evidenced though it may be true. There is no comparison to make this conclusion. There is not evidence of liver damage occur when training and fasting thus B cannot be concluded from the information provided.

Stress is not mentioned in the table and cannot be reliably concluded.

However since the only information provided for a high CHO diet indicates an increase when training then C is correct.

Question 11

A

It is not clear, though it may be implied, that human activity is the cause of the increase thus B must be negated. The data does not track CO_2 levels for the past five million years thus C can also be negated. There is no way a reliable prediction can be made about possible future CO_2 concentrations thus D is incorrect.

It can only be reliably concluded from the graph that CO_2 levels have peaked in the period since 1958. Thus A is correct.

Question 12

D

The distance between successive rises and falls in CO_2 is in the order of 10ppm, thus A is incorrect. CO_2 levels do seem to rise and fall in predictable patterns thus B is not correct. From the data presented it cannot be concluded that CO_2 levels contribute to global warming – there is no evidence to link the two in the data presented.

It should be clear that CO_2 levels rise and fall in a pattern thus D is correct.

Question 13

D

In order to manage exercise induced-anaphylaxis several things are suggested in the text including varying diet, reducing the level of exercise and the use of antihistamines. There is no suggestion that low intensity exercises should be performed. Thus D is correct in that it is the only option that is NOT in the information.

Question 14

C

Though several factors have been identified it cannot be concluded that only four factors are responsible for exercise-induced anaphylaxis there A is not correct. It is not suggested that people should not eat prior to exercise so B can be discounted. It also does not follow that itchy skin must occur after strong exercise thus D is also incorrect.

It is the case that people with exercise-induced anaphylaxis can get lumps under the skin ('cutaneous signs').

Question 15

D

The text suggests that the two conditions manifest similar symptoms but does not suggest that cholinergic urticarial occurs as a result of exercise, nor is there a suggestion that that particular condition and exercise-induced anaphylaxis be managed through the use of an epipen. Thus A and B can be ruled out. Since A is incorrect it follows that C must also be incorrect.

The text suggests that both have similar symptoms and careful diagnosis therefore needs to be made. Hence D is correct.

Question 16

A

The statistics quoted do not suggest such the high mortality rate suggested in B. It is not clear from the data presented whether Type 2 diabetes or ischaemic heart disease is more prevalent hence C can be ruled out. 30% of the rise in diabetes has come from obesity AND other risk factors hence D is wrong.

70% of the increase in diabetes has been attributed to aging populations and 44% of the diabetes burden comes from obesity (BMI greater than 30) hence A is correct.

Question 17

C

Insulin sensitivity is often low in people with obesity but it is not always the case hence A is not correct. There is nothing in the text to suggest that Type-2 diabetes is treated with drugs that adapt to insulin hence B is not correct. There is also nothing in the text that suggests increased insulin sensitivity will overcome diabetes in thin mice.

It should be clear from the text that the removal of T-bet has led to increased insulin sensitivity thus the research is looking at how to develop on this. Hence C is correct.

Question 18

C

Nowhere is it suggested that a BMI of under 25 is either healthy or unhealthy hence A is not correct. Treating the cause of obesity may possible affect the incidence of some cancers hence B may be possible. However it does not follow that it would do so. The relationship between obesity and ischaemic heart disease in mice is not referred to thus D cannot be ruled in.

However, if obesity is defined as a proportion of weight to height: kg/m^2 then $40kg/1^2$ = a BMI of 40 and hence is obese thus C is correct.

Question 19

B

The number of females is 2,400. There must therefore be 3,600 males. Of these 1,620 work in factories and of the 2,400 females 480 work in offices. 2,400 adults own cars meaning that 3,600 do not own cars.

1,800 adults own cars and work in factories or offices – hence 600 adults own cars and do not work in factories or offices – thus B is correct.

Question 20

D

80% of 6,000 is 4,800. From the answer in 19 it can be seen that 1,620 males work in factories and 480 females work in offices. This totals 2,100 people. 2,100/4,800 = 7/16 or D. Note: an assumption here is made that no males work in offices and that no females work in factories.

Question 21

C

There is no evidence to suggest that pigeons would be disorientated as a result of expose to electricity thus A can be ruled out. Whilst magnetite has been found on the beaks of pigeons it does not follow that they must eat diets with iron to fly home thus B is not correct. Similarly, if pigeons eat bees then it cannot be assumed the magnetite in bees would become magnetite in pigeons, hence D is not correct.

Solar flares disrupt normal magnetic fields and thus require a period of adaptation. It can be concluded that during the period of change/adaptation normal flight will be disrupted hence C is correct.

Question 22

A

The text does not suggest pain receptors and trophocytes are matched hence B is incorrect. The text does not discuss whether the nervous system can act independently of trophocytes thus D must be cross out. Moreover, the trophocytes are not to work with the circulatory system but do seem to interact with the nervous system hence A is correct.

Question 23

A

Whilst camels may be a 'protein resource' they are not a source of food for Australians thus D is not correct. There is no suggestion that Aboriginal communities must learn to manage feral camels thus C is also incorrect. The central issue is that of a disparate approach to the problem by the states. Hence, the states need to align in order to effectively manage the issue – so A is correct and B is not.

Question 24

B

The text is not specific about the damage caused by camels to infrastructure except to say 'fences' thus D is not correct. The text is also not detailed enough for a reader to determine whether the stakeholders (pastoralists, government and Indigenous Australians) have differing approaches thus C is not correct either.

Whilst feral camels have some negative impacts they are far from overwhelming. Moreover, properly managed camels can lead to economic benefits – thus A is incorrect and B is correct.

Question 25

C

Marriage rates have fluctuated (see decline in 2004) thus A is not correct. Divorces peaked in 2001 but marriage rates appear to be rising. Indeed in 2001 marriage rates were at their lowest thus B is not correct. During 2008 – 2010 divorce rates actual rose thus D is not correct. From the graphs however C is correct – with marriage rates rising above 199 levels in 2008.

Question 26

B

Divorces were lower in 1991 than 2011 thus A is not correct. The number of divorces was 48,935 and the number of marriages was 121,752. Clearly the number of individuals divorcing is far lower than the number marrying (double both numbers) thus C is not correct. The number of couples that married in 2010 was 121,176 – thus 576 more couple married thus D is incorrect too. In 2011 it can be seen that marriage registrations are rising (as they have since mid-2005) and divorce rates are falling as they have been since 2010.

Question 27

D

The marriage rates in 2001 were the lowest in the decade but no comment can be made about whether it was the lowest 'on record' thus B is not correct. 2001 represents peaks and troughs thus C can be eliminated. Out of A and D the latter is correct and A in NOT correct because divorce rates peaked and have fallen since.

Question 28

D

Between 2001 and 2006 Marriage rates rose and fell and divorce rates peaked and fell thus A is not true. The number of females aged 30 in *de facto* relationships is significantly higher than the number of males aged 25 (see lines on the graph) thus B is not correct. No correlation can be drawn from a point in time graph of *de facto* relationships and the trends in divorce and marriages shown thus C is not correct.

The date says that there were 1,193,400 *de facto* relationships in 2006and from the graphs the number of marriages was 115,000 and the number of divorces 51,600 thus D is correct.

Question 29

C

Veno-arteriolar reflex is caused by constriction of the blood vessels not dilation thus A is not correct. The reflex does not automatically occur hence B is not correct either. To detect orthostatic interference a Xenon tracer is used not a sterile solution thus D is incorrect. The text says that astronauts experience orthostatic intolerance upon re-entry – thus the vessels are not properly constricting hence C is correct.

Question 30

D

Blotchiness is not mentioned thus A is not correct. Dizziness and fainting are mentioned but migranes and hearing loss are not thus B and C can be ruled out and D is correct.

Question 31

A

36.6 grams is 2 biscuits or 2 serves. Thus it would equate to 2 x4.6% of the daily energy intake (left hand side of the table) which is just over 9%.

Question 32

B

3 serves would weigh 54.9 grams and would provide 3 x 1.3 = 3.9% of daily sodium therefore A can be eliminated. 3 serves would provide 3 x 7.0% = 21% or just over one-fifth of daily total fat and also 3.8 x 3 or 11.4% of carbohydrate hence C is not correct. 3 serves would provide 29mg x 3 = 87mg of sodium thus D is not correct.

3 serves would $^3/_{11}$ of the package or 27.3% and would provide 3 x 8.1g of sugars or 24.3g thus B is correct.

Question 33

D

The Indigenous Australians understood climate in terms of huge variations and used descriptive terms. Thus A is clearly incorrect as is C. The terms they applied to describe climate included humid, fog, rainfall, frosty, early and late rains thus B is not correct. Across tribal groups and zones there ware between 3 and 7 seasons identified – thus D is correct.

Question 34

B

The two groups had every different climate descriptors thus A is incorrect. They do both describe December as wet but September is called "Hot' by the Mirriwoong and is classified as cold, dry and dusty by the Yawuru – hence C is incorrect. Neither of the groups follow similar climate classifications as the Yanyuwa and though the Mirriwoong classification is quite similar to that of the Walabunba it is still at variance.

In reality B is correct as both groups live in different regions of Western Australia and both classify the climate quite differently.

Question 35

B

A is not correct as six months after the start of the Marrai'gang the climate is cool getting warmer. C is not correct, as three months after the start of the Wunthurru it is wet season with heavy rainfall. D is also not correct as four months after the end of the Ngoonungi it is hot and dry.

Four months before the start of the Wujerrijin the Wardaman peoples describe the climate as being between November and December thus it is hot and wet so B is correct.

Question 36

B

At a depth of 35 metres underwater can lead to hypothermia but it will not lead to decompression thus A is wrong. A diver is not a risk of death unless they run out of air and thus C is not correct. The level of oxygen dissolved in the blood will rise and this will be used by tissues so it is not clear when the oxygen level will fall thus D is partially, but not fully correct. B is the best answer as at depth a diver can get nitrogen narcosis and thus can feel drowsy and euphoric.

Question 37

A

Nitrogen narcosis and residual nitrogen are only a problem if a person rises too quickly and thus do not, of themselves, cause heart attack, stroke or ruptured blood vessels, thus B is not correct. Rapidly ascending would be disasterous and could kill thus do not manage the issue hence C is incorrect.

Whilst a decompression chamber may be required to overcome the effects of nitrogen narcosis and residual nitrogen in the event of rapid ascension, it is not necessary if a person decreases dive depth through ascending slowly. Thus D is incorrect and A is correct.

Question 38

C

There is no risk of compression and decompression if diving is managed well thus A is not correct. The effect of diving at depth is not to numb the lungs thus B is also not correct. The tingling sensation described is a result of rapid decompression not nitrogen narcosis thus D is not correct. Clearly, careful management of diving depths requires managing the level of dissolved nitrogen and managing a limited air supply that may require a person to rise too quickly to the surface thus C is correct.

Question 39

B

There is no suggestion that rain increases the range of the frog to over 4 metres thus A is not correct. The frog rarely bred more than once in a season and this was due to brooding times not rainfall, thus C is ruled out. As juveniles did move between pools then D is eliminated.

B is correct as breeding activity is dependent upon summer rains.

Question 40

A

There is no suggestion that the tadpoles would form groups thus B is eliminated. As the tadpoles were expelled from the mother's mouth as young frogs then C must be incorrect. Moreover, as they lived and grew in the mother's stomach they could not have moved very far thus D is incorrect.

As the tadpoles were in the mother's stomach the mother had adapted to produce hormones that would stop her from digesting her own young – thus A is correct.

Question 41

C

Breathing pure oxygen will assist in the creation of hydrogen peroxide but this does not bleach infection to kill it thus A is incorrect. The use of pure oxygen assists cancer appears to assist in circulation thus may assist cancer sufferers and those with diabetes. The creation of healing scaffolds is a separate process and thus B is incorrect. Whilst oxygen can assist in the repair and growth of blood vessels it cannot be concluded that it will do so thus D is not correct. However, C is correct as it takes this view and correctly states that it 'encourages the capacity for...repair'.

Question 42

D

There is no link between at what depths wounds occurred and what can or cannot be treated thus A is wrong. There is also no suggestion that wound healing will take place up to 15 times faster hence B is incorrect. It does not follow that wounds not healing through conventional means would heal with HBOT thus C can be eliminated.

HBOT involves delivering oxygen at pressure 2.0 – 2.4 times higher than the pressure at sea level and this can deliver oxygen at 15 times the normal level thus D is the best response.

Question 43

A

Nowhere does it state that joint cells attack immune cells thus B is patently incorrect. There is no evidence to suggest that a healthy immune system will of itself fight of pancreatitis thus C must be ruled out. Inflammation can come from many sources including a knock thus D is clearly incorrect.

A is correct as celiac is an autoimmune disease and the characteristic of such diseases is the body's cytotoxic cells attacking the body's tissues.

Question 44

C

Protective immunity is the opposite to autoimmunity thus A is not right. B is not correct as the cytotoxic cells need to kill the antigens for an effective immune response. D is clearly not correct as each of the toxins listed would be killed in a healthy body.

C is correct as the TSH produced is meant to fight off disease but the body creates antibodies to this chemical thus attacking its own immune response.

Question 45

B

As the winds shift from the South to the Southeast then A is incorrect. That is, the wind is shifting East. There is precipitation forecast from Monday through to Thursday with a break on Wednesday so C is incorrect. Humidity will rise when there is a combination of rainfall and warmth – this rules out Sunday and thus D is incorrect.

Hence B is correct as the winds shift more Easterly and the amount of precipitation rises through the week.

Question 46

C

The dates run from Friday the 31st May to Thursday 6th June – all before the summer solstice on 22nd June. The days are therefore getting longer. Thus A, B and D are all incorrect as they either shorten the day or keep the days the same length.

C is correct.

Question 47

C

Service closures were higher in 2011 than the closures of finance businesses thus A is incorrect. Since it is not clear why the business closures occurred (there may or may not have been an economic downturn) then B cannot be concluded. Mining and manufacturing firms did no go against trend in 2011 as public administration, agriculture and wholesale were all flat and finance fell. Prior to that mining had fluctuated thus to look at either trend demonstrates that D is not correct.

Adding the number of failures in 2009 gives:

Agriculture (40) + Construction (640) + Finance (1,200) + Manufacturing (500) + Mining (20) + Public Admin (10) + Retail (400) + Services (900) + Transportation (160) + Wholesale (360) = 4,230 which is greater than 4,000 and therefore correct.

Question 48

A

There is no mention of the cost of set up hence B can be ruled out. C makes no sense. There is no mention of the number of businesses failing as a comparison between large and small, thus D cannot be concluded.

Small business start-ups fell by 95% thus it is clear that fewer people are prepared to set up their own business and A is correct.

Essential Preparation for

UMAT

UNDERGRADUATE MEDICINE & HEALTH SCIENCES ADMISSION TEST

MULTIPLE CHOICE ANSWER SHEET

1	(A) (B) (C) (D)	25	(A) (B) (C) (D)
2	(A) (B) (C) (D)	26	(A) (B) (C) (D)
3	(A) (B) (C) (D)	27	(A) (B) (C) (D)
4	(A) (B) (C) (D)	28	(A) (B) (C) (D)
5	(A) (B) (C) (D)	29	(A) (B) (C) (D)
6	(A) (B) (C) (D)	30	(A) (B) (C) (D)
7	(A) (B) (C) (D)	31	(A) (B) (C) (D)
8	(A) (B) (C) (D)	32	(A) (B) (C) (D)
9	(A) (B) (C) (D)	33	(A) (B) (C) (D)
10	(A) (B) (C) (D)	34	(A) (B) (C) (D)
11	(A) (B) (C) (D)	35	(A) (B) (C) (D)
12	(A) (B) (C) (D)	36	(A) (B) (C) (D)
13	(A) (B) (C) (D)	37	(A) (B) (C) (D)
14	(A) (B) (C) (D)	38	(A) (B) (C) (D)
15	(A) (B) (C) (D)	39	(A) (B) (C) (D)
16	(A) (B) (C) (D)	40	(A) (B) (C) (D)
17	(A) (B) (C) (D)	41	(A) (B) (C) (D)
18	(A) (B) (C) (D)	42	(A) (B) (C) (D)
19	(A) (B) (C) (D)	43	(A) (B) (C) (D)
20	(A) (B) (C) (D)	44	(A) (B) (C) (D)
21	(A) (B) (C) (D)	45	(A) (B) (C) (D)
22	(A) (B) (C) (D)	46	(A) (B) (C) (D)
23	(A) (B) (C) (D)	47	(A) (B) (C) (D)
24	(A) (B) (C) (D)	48	(A) (B) (C) (D)

Essential Preparation for
UMAT
UNDERGRADUATE MEDICINE & HEALTH SCIENCES ADMISSION TEST
MULTIPLE CHOICE ANSWER SHEET

Use pencil when filling out this sheet

Fill in the circle correctly			
●	B	C	D

If you make a mistake neatly cross it out and circle the correct response			
✗	●	C	D

1 Ⓐ Ⓑ Ⓒ Ⓓ
2 Ⓐ Ⓑ Ⓒ Ⓓ
3 Ⓐ Ⓑ Ⓒ Ⓓ
4 Ⓐ Ⓑ Ⓒ Ⓓ
5 Ⓐ Ⓑ Ⓒ Ⓓ
6 Ⓐ Ⓑ Ⓒ Ⓓ
7 Ⓐ Ⓑ Ⓒ Ⓓ
8 Ⓐ Ⓑ Ⓒ Ⓓ
9 Ⓐ Ⓑ Ⓒ Ⓓ
10 Ⓐ Ⓑ Ⓒ Ⓓ
11 Ⓐ Ⓑ Ⓒ Ⓓ
12 Ⓐ Ⓑ Ⓒ Ⓓ
13 Ⓐ Ⓑ Ⓒ Ⓓ
14 Ⓐ Ⓑ Ⓒ Ⓓ
15 Ⓐ Ⓑ Ⓒ Ⓓ
16 Ⓐ Ⓑ Ⓒ Ⓓ
17 Ⓐ Ⓑ Ⓒ Ⓓ
18 Ⓐ Ⓑ Ⓒ Ⓓ
19 Ⓐ Ⓑ Ⓒ Ⓓ
20 Ⓐ Ⓑ Ⓒ Ⓓ
21 Ⓐ Ⓑ Ⓒ Ⓓ
22 Ⓐ Ⓑ Ⓒ Ⓓ
23 Ⓐ Ⓑ Ⓒ Ⓓ
24 Ⓐ Ⓑ Ⓒ Ⓓ

25 Ⓐ Ⓑ Ⓒ Ⓓ
26 Ⓐ Ⓑ Ⓒ Ⓓ
27 Ⓐ Ⓑ Ⓒ Ⓓ
28 Ⓐ Ⓑ Ⓒ Ⓓ
29 Ⓐ Ⓑ Ⓒ Ⓓ
30 Ⓐ Ⓑ Ⓒ Ⓓ
31 Ⓐ Ⓑ Ⓒ Ⓓ
32 Ⓐ Ⓑ Ⓒ Ⓓ
33 Ⓐ Ⓑ Ⓒ Ⓓ
34 Ⓐ Ⓑ Ⓒ Ⓓ
35 Ⓐ Ⓑ Ⓒ Ⓓ
36 Ⓐ Ⓑ Ⓒ Ⓓ
37 Ⓐ Ⓑ Ⓒ Ⓓ
38 Ⓐ Ⓑ Ⓒ Ⓓ
39 Ⓐ Ⓑ Ⓒ Ⓓ
40 Ⓐ Ⓑ Ⓒ Ⓓ
41 Ⓐ Ⓑ Ⓒ Ⓓ
42 Ⓐ Ⓑ Ⓒ Ⓓ
43 Ⓐ Ⓑ Ⓒ Ⓓ
44 Ⓐ Ⓑ Ⓒ Ⓓ
45 Ⓐ Ⓑ Ⓒ Ⓓ
46 Ⓐ Ⓑ Ⓒ Ⓓ
47 Ⓐ Ⓑ Ⓒ Ⓓ
48 Ⓐ Ⓑ Ⓒ Ⓓ